" Tweeting Through Time"

Soulful serenade of wings and memories...

Babita Sharma

BookLeaf Publishing

India | USA | UK

Made with ❤ on the BookLeaf Publishing Platform
www.bookleafpub.in
www.bookleafpub.com

Dedication

To those, who seek solace in words and those who have walked with me in the gardens of life sharing laughter,tears and everyday moments of joy that shape us.

To all the wonderful feathered creatures who grace the skies and whose songs echo through the tapestry of our lives.
This collection is a tribute - A Celebration of the wild , the fleeting and the sacred echoes of the heart.
May the words within, inspire anyone who chooses to read this book to take flight and soar with open wings .

Preface

In our collective human experience, few subjects evoke
the same sense of wonder and connection as the avian
inhabitants of our skies. Birds with their remarkable
diversity and ethereal beauty, have long captured our
imagination, symbolizing freedom, transformation, and
the fleeting nature of life. From the soft shrill of a
morning warbler to the majestic flight of an eagle, these
winged creatures inspire   reflect and reverberate with us
humans in so many ways.

This book, a unique fusion of poetry and memories,
seeks to explore the intricate relationship between birds ,
nature and our personal journeys. The resonant verses
and intimate stories, have woven a   a path of discovery
—one where the simplicity of a bird's song can
intertwine with the complexities of our lives.

Each poem serves as a bridge, connecting experiences of
longing, love, loss, and hope to the natural world that
exists just outside our windows. The memories
complement these verses, offering glimpses into the
moments when birds became symbols of solace or
reminders of our own paths. They are invitations to
pause and reflect, to listen to the whispers of the wings

around us, and to consider how these encounters with nature shape our own narratives.

Within these pages, you will find a symphony of voices, each contributing their melody to a larger chorus of understanding. As you immerse yourself in the words, I encourage you to embrace the stillness and the chaos of your own life, allowing the presence of birds to illuminate your memories, ruminate your thoughts, and inspire a deeper connection with the world around you.

May this collection of poems and memories nourish your spirit and remind you of the beauty found in both the delicate flutter of a feathered friend and the profound stories we carry within us. In a world often too busy to pause and reflect, let us take flight together—one word, one memory, one bird at a time to find the solace one longs for, in life.

Acknowledgements

As I bring this collection pf poems to life , my heart swells with gratitude for the close ones who have nurtured my passion for writing and deepened my appreciation for the beauty of the natural world.
First and foremost I thank my avian visitors for enticing me with their beauty,their songs ,their flights They remind me of their resilience and grace with each flutter they make and the sequence of life that connects us all.

To my family ,specially my husband who put up with my difficult demands and allowing me to do things my way, with a lot of patience.To you, my elder son who initiated bird watching and made me fall in love with the winged beauties. To my younger son & his wife Prerita ,for lending me an ear for a patient hearing of my compositions.

To all others whose presence in my life , encouraged and made me embrace and delve in to my memoirs and experiences .
Lastly to the readers who hold this book in their hands :thank you for venturing in to the world of my words. It is my sincerest hope that these poems resonate with you and strike a chord with your own journey through life.

With gratitude,
Babita Sharma

1. Lessons: by tailor bird

"O Mommy if I take the lead I fear, I'll fall;"
Said, the baby bird to it's mommy on the wall,
Nah! Don't you fear my baby dear;
I promise to hold you & always be near,
One must take the risk & endure;
Then the success will be yours, I ensure,
So baby, open your wings & take the chance;
Only then in life will you advance!
The lil birdie then gathered some courage & shook its wings,
 Mummy, I'm nervous but I'll take this chance & see, what it brings.
And so, the little one then took its maiden flight;
While the mother edged it with all its might,
But alas the birdie landed on the thorns!
The beautiful rose plant adorned,
And the tweets of the duo became quite shrill;
The mother tweeted as if, seemed to instil,
"My dear, watch your step! As life is not a bed of roses,
You have to deal with the threat it poses".
As if understood it all, the little one chirped loudly!
And flapped its soft wings ever so proudly,
Once more it flew to land on the grill;

It hopped around in glee as if it understood the drill,
The mother from a distance watched her baby grow that day;
Assured it was, that now it can fend for itself and find its way,
I sat bewildered and amused at today's little star!
 And the fact that how So much like us these birdies are!!!

2. Nature - A perfect seamstress !

While the grey hornbills are busy painting the town
red......
Hidden in a corner was this Great barbet!

A symphony of colors suddenly arises;
 Perched on the tree ,bewitches & hypnotizes.
The hues , the proportions, the range of shades ;
 Somewhere a color dominates while another fades....

 Such marvels can only be God's creations!
And man ? Oh he just lives on its plagiarisation !

The perfect fashion designer and seamstress;
  Who else is? But our mother goddess!

 A "blanket of wool" knitted so pretty;
For coining the name , thank you dear sis, Iti,
 This cascade of colors on display ;
 Great Barbet u really made my day!
  With new hope & a new song to sing ;
 Hope all will be well in the world this Spring!!

3. BIRDS! BIRDS & BIRDS-1

As the rain stops & out comes the sun;
The world of birds is back on the run,
A swarm of flies ,bees & wasps dot the sky;
Out come these hunters too ,who can somersault high!
Its feasting time for the bee eaters blue & green;
Perched on wires, Whistling & chirping these can be
seen,
A hint of green,gold & shades of blue;
These pretty glistening birds with majestic hues,
With crimson iris & a line of kohl across the eye;
Are these to charm the prey ,which is passing by?
Posing pretty,these little balls of wool ,drying on the
wire;
Such stunning is their attire , one can't help but admire!
Although the mornings are slothful, just to huddle
&cuddle ;
But surprisingly for numerous dives , their energy
is quintuple!
Erratic dashes these dainty birds make to grab their prey;
And come back to the same perch is their feeding way,
The blue bearded bee eater with a turquoise gleam;
Which glows even more with the falling sun beam,

Bends its body like a bow & arrow for a sure short aim;
'Sharnga or Vishnu's Bow" is also its name,
As the rain stops & out comes the sun;
Well! the list of such birds has just begun,
A swarm of flies ,bees & wasps dot the sky;
Out come these hunters too ,who can somersault high!
In a sequel I'll present these birds to you.....;
Stay tuned friends! for the next rendezvous......,
Every time I see the birds, spellbound! I am at his creation!
I bow my head in pure reverence & admiration,
To the one, capable of such variation ,compilation & Collation!
To the Supreme power, which runs this constellation!!

4. BIRDS ! BIRDS & BIRDS -2

As the rain stops & out comes the sun;
The world of birds is back on the run,
Today's bird was the first to fly from Noah's Arc, much
ahead of the pack;
It then ,caught the blue of the sky on its back,
And on the breast , fell the orange of the setting sun;
With dagger like beaks & binocular vision ,
The little blue magicians hunt with precision,
The bird 'HALCYON' in Greek mythology;
Is known to possess powers to calm the sea,
'Halcyon days', is a phrase ,attributed to the kingfishers'
Which usher in nostalgic memories of yesteryear's,
Birds have always been an integral part;
Of man's life since the start,
In fables, folklore ,as symbols & messenger of peace;
Right from India to Macedonia & Greece,
These feathered marvels were added to our world with a
purpose;
To learn ,adapt, add fun & colors to Our life, I suppose!
And while you marvel at this blue & golden wonder;
Next on my list is a distant cousin,known for its crown &
colorful splendor!

So next , be ready to be swooned by this
bird's grandeur!!

5. BIRDS ! BIRDS & BIRDS-3

One afternoon , as the rain stopped & out came the sun;
The sound of "OOP!OOP!OOP",drew my attention,
And guess who had made an entry?
there! the" Hoopie", was perched right in front of me!
In a gown of fawn ,white & brown it was dressed;
This royal beauty ,with a feathered crown on it's head ,

In flight, it resembles a giant butterfly;
Oh & to woo the female! you should see ,what all they try!
The males of this species, surely know the way to the lady's heart!
And if the 'Nuptial gift ' of worms is accepted,soon a family will start!

As I enthrall you with it's grandeur;
The charisma of this bird will surely enamor,

Besides the title of " National bird of Israel", to it's name;
Hoopie has so much more, on the list of fame,
Was revered & considered sacred in ancient Egypt;
So, on the tomb & temple walls it was depicted,
It was a symbolic code, by which the heir was predicted;

In the biblical tale of queen Sheeba & king Solomen,
To queen Sheeba ,"Hoopie " carried the king's royal
invitation;
As a symbol of virtue in Persia, it is known;
In "Minion Crete" too, Its importance is shown,

This humble woodpecker , a part of our childhood
memories;
I realize, has been around for many a centuries,
Each time,that I read a tale or a folklore;
I am mesmerized by these birdies, a little more,
The quest for a picture then seeps in ;
And that's how a new tale begins!

6. " The Thrush "

And what a morning this was!
To be woken up by the song of the Thrush,
On my window was this bird of mystery ;
 And when I read about it ,was with quite a history !
 In Greek mythology King Pansdion , of Athens had
two daughters ;

 The elder Proxne and Philomela , her dear younger
sister.
 Proxne was married to king Tereus ;
 When Philomela went to visit her sister, things turned
ugly and serious ,
  During the return voyage, his lust for the younger
one;
 Made Threce assault Philomela abandon her in the
woods, when it was done ,
 Philomela was defiant and this angered Tereus, who cut
her tongue .

 She was wounded gravely & wove a tapestry ;   Which
depicted the horror of her misery ,
 She then sent it to Procne, her sister ; Upon learning the
inhuman deeds of his mister,

Procne killed and cooked their son Itys and served to
her husband;
  On learning the truth ,Tereus wanted both the
sisters life to end,
He then ran with an with an axe to kill ;
  While sisters prayed to god to escape from the
clutches of the devil,

Who transformed Procne in to a swallow and Philomila
into a nightingale;
  And t his is how goes the ,Greek thrush tale!   The
beauty and inspiration of this thrush does not end here !
If interested? read on further my dear,

  Robert Browning in " Home thoughts from abroad
," refers to it as the wise thrush but so sober.
   Who ,to express the power of recapture , repeats   each
song twice over ,

  Then says Thomas Hardy, in his " Darkling Thrush ", the
joyful song of the thrush so dear ;
  In the middle of gloom brings some hope and cheer,

  In "The Thrush "Edward Thomas says; And
comprehends it in his own ways ,
  Though it is frail, gaunt and small; But does it sing in

happy moments or without any reason at all ?

 William Words worth in "The Tables Turned" says ,let
nature be a teacher;
 And the Thursh be our preacher .
 All over the world clubs, hotels & motels rush ;
 To keep their name as "The Thrush",

 It's melodious voice I could not record & will wait for
another lucky day ;
 When this beautiful , tiny little song bird will again ,
cross my way !

7. A Peekaboo in to the Babbler World!

So identical are the birds of the same species;
As, Its just the Jungle babbler , what the human eye sees,
Then how do these birds recognize?
Who is the husband & who is, whose wife?
which child was fed in the first go ?
Coz, to me, all kids appear the same when sitting on a
bough;
I sometimes wonder, do these birds too,have traits &
nicknames like us?
"Sona. Raja,Tannu ,Mannu"do they call each other thus?

My chain of thoughts was broken by a flock of noisy
babblers;
These chattering, chirping,squeaking ramblers,
Named as' Seven Sisters or Seven Brothers';
When around give two hoots to others!
Was it a display of power & muscle?
On the premonition of a tussle?
See the video and let me know;
Was it, just a gimmick & a show?

On the same tree a flame back, was busy drilling a hole;
Perhaps! Looking for termites was the goal,

Could bear their shrill no longer& shooed the sentinel
away;
But babblers being babblers , were here to stay!
They hopped on to a nearby tree;,
And continued... their cacophony spree,

And as if drawn by the noise in town;
This bird with a glistening crown & wings of cinnamon
brown ,
Came to check what the fuss was all about?
Oh! It is the Paradise flycatcher,without a doubt!

On seeing the babblers were on an outing;
This was the reason for all the shouting!
Flew away flycatcher& the flame back ;
To take on another journey on a new track,

Seeing all this brought a smile to my lips;
And now it was time for me, to string the bits,
Of the drama that unfolded today;
For keepsakes to look back another day!!

8. Monsoon And Little Things !!

Sighting of the Jacobin Cuckoo ,is the harbinger;
Monsoons are soon approaching ,it whispers,
Mythology too, has a mention of Jacobin's name;
In Kalidasa's Meghadoot, as" Chataka"it has earned its fame,
A ray of hope for the farmer's standing crops;
The parched land eager to soak in ,the raindrops,
Let peace seep in to you , this rain ;
Let the child in you, bloom once again,
Remember! the paper boats we made & then set them sail!
Watching ,who the winner would be at the end of the trail?
The deliberate splash in the puddle & the wet shoes;
The almost brown shirts& forgotten mother's don'ts & do's ,
O man! Awaken from the melee of life & notice;
The misty windows,bearing the impression of the breathing breeze,
The clouds hanging low ,as if hugging & kissing the trees;
The earthy scent of the soil after the first showers of rain,

Which ,then will forever in your senses remain;
The magnificent changing shades of the skies,
Such a blissful treat to man's tired eyes;
 Mushrooms & wild daisies decorate the earth,
As if announcing & rejoicing ,their birth;
The rain-kissed flowers & the sparkling greener grass,
Drops holding on to the tip of leaves & unpredictable
showers;
Let these sparkles hold on to your hair too;
Dance In the rain &let romance sweep you two,
Its time, to rediscover the lost- you, in this hullabaloo;
Do these little things often , that a child would do,
Let the soul breathe, rejoice &refresh itself;
Take out & read that book , lying for so long, on the
shelf,
With my black diary & old melodies playing in the
background;
Sipping hot cuppa & some fries, gives me joy profound,
Give an ear to the-pitter-patter of the raindrops & see,
what they have to say?
They say,"We make music while you dance your way!"
Build some memories & tuck them in your heart;
These rainy days will help you ,make a good start,
For you to rewind & look back one day ;
Blessed were you to have lived that way!
Live life & enjoy simple pleasures as it is cascading so
fast ;

Coz, your goodness, noble deeds & memories only ,will forever ,last!!

17

9. Summer days at Grandma's place!

Summer days at Grandma's place,are a few of my treasured memories;
Green pastures,Aam- baag,paddy fields & the green custard apple trees,
The narrow brook,the grazing cows & the gentle flowing breeze;
Chirping birds,butterflies & the humming honey bees,
The fascination with the tailor bird was, perhaps born then as a child ;
The" DARZEE" in Rudyard Kipling's Jungle Book was what always kept me beguiled!!
Intricately stitched leaves were works of wonder for me;
I am sure, these things must have filled your hearts too, with glee,
Baya's hanging retorts were next on my fascination list;
Does a more stunning marvel of wooing exist?
Then there is a bird named Oriental eye;
Look at the picture & you'll know why?
The Green bee-eater,yellow breasted warbler,Grey breasted prinia & the Crimson sun birds;
On beauty & expertise of these petite little birds ,I fall short of words,
Chiwee- chiwee,Chip-Chip-Chip,USee-Usee,Which-

Which-Which!!!
Do give an ear & try to see & listen;
To the bounty of nature with a medley of whistles,
Come on dear friends & let the child in U, sing along;
And dance a little to the tunes of these tiny birds' song!!!

10. PICKLES - Nostalgia In Bottles...

Pickles, tangy mango chutney, Aloo chips & Urad Vadis,
kindle the nostalgic flame;
Every Summer, these things take me down the memory
lane,
All these, transcend me to my grandma's place;
So fresh are those precious childhood days,
The daily veranda chit -chat on the cane moorahs during
the lazy afternoon;
Listening to her tales was itself a boon,
How masi's finger got cut on a swing;
& how mum, the darling wasn't allowed to do a thing!
Be it the scent of the fresh cut grass;
Or the freshly churned buttermilk glass,
Be it the wild yellow flowers blooming in the meadows
nearby;
Or the garlic & the mangoes drying under the sky;
Perhaps! a new savory was coming by!
My Nani , a tiny lady but surely a wonder woman;
Such wisdom! about all things from where did she
acumen?
May be, she learnt from her mother in her own ways;
After all those were not the YOU TUBE Days!!

The texture, the taste& the scent of Aam Ka Achaar;
The room ,the attic & the porcelain jars,
Entry in this room for us was forbidden;
As it was here , the goodies were stored for all her children,
Each visit she would pack our share of delicacies & pickles;
The taste of which to date on my palate trickles,
Wish I had some foresight in those times;
Would have surely jotted these lost recipes in a few lines,
My pickles, Nani are a little tribute to U in my own way;
To show that love for U is etched in our hearts & will forever stay,
Till date before beginning any process;
I remember U ,MY CULINARY GODDESS!
Two magical components .I learnt from U are Love & Care;
A ladle of both and one can prepare,
The most sumptuous of dishes;
That every heart so desires & wishes!!

11. TIME & TIDE- waits for none;

TIME & TIDE waits for no one;
Reminds, both,the clock & the waves of the ocean,
Every passing second teaches;
let go! of ego,petty issues & hatred it preaches,
The rat race to reach the top;
This insanity & Amassing must stop,
Its time to pause,rewind & cleanse our soul;
Imbibe empathy,satisfaction& drink happiness from life's bowl,
The meandering river , the gentle breeze & buds waiting to pop & bloom;
all beckoning U to recon & set aside the gloom,
The Plum headed parakeet with myriad hues as on a painter's palate;
Colors all strewn, as if narrating a ballad,
The greater Coucal with coppery brown wings;
Coog ! Coog! Coog! is it's cackle or is this how it sings?
The harbinger of fortune & a good omen to be spotted;
 Many myths & folklore to its name, are dotted,
The repetitive chorus, Did he do it !! Did he do it! of the Red wattled Lapwing;
And to watch the drop dead act of its chicks, Is surely a thing!

Well ! for happiness one doesn't require worldly possessions & wealth;
All that counts is Family, friends, happiness & health,
Flip Ur life around & make a fresh start;
Appreciate little things & let songs of love fill your heart,
Every dusk holds promises of a new dawn,says the hour glass!
Let's , till then hold hands and this too shall pass!!

12. Nature's Silence

Nature's Silence too conveys;
Of the oncoming time & days,
See carefully & it will unfold;
No words spoken but volumes told,
Through the changing color of leaves;
Then these falling with the breeze,
Through the flowers so bright, against the skies;
Enticing the humming bees & dancing butterflies,
Through these flowers turning to fruits;
And these fruits leaving seeds behind, in the pursuit ;
Of new progeny, arising from the shoots,
Through the waves kissing the seashore;
Telling us to Learn ,imbibe & explore,
Through the shifting rays of the sun;
This day & time is already on the run,
Through the bite of chill in the air ;
Winter is knocking at the door,so better prepare,
Through the ants & Squirrels stocking for adverse
climate;
As they know it'll soon be time to hibernate,
Through the festivals ,ushering in hope & new
beginnings;
Telling us , to rejoice there are a million things!!
Let this lesson be learnt by the human clan;

We are all here as a part of an eternal plan ,
A mere speck in this vast universe;
On some preset path we traverse,
So why brood, envy & complain?
From hatred & malice, we must abstain,
Through Nature's Silence we must learn;
Each thing ,Each one has its own time & turn,
And when we reach the celestial gate;
Our karma will decide OUR fate!!

13. THE TALE OF THE JACARANDA TREE !

Hi ! I am the Jacaranda Tree!
In bloom ,at Su -Satya B-233,
Today let me , to you, bare my heart ;
& narrate my story from the start,
When these people purchased the land;
First the contractor wanted to uproot my stand,
Next, on me they hung electric wires like a garland;
Scars & burns it's then, I acquired;
Looks I bore, no one admired,

The lady of the house then came one day;
Saw all this and said," No Way!"
"Right now!Remove this and let the tree breathe;
Water it daily till it gets back its sheath",
She ordered, as she caressed my burns;
Off she walked then, between the ferns,
Her gentle touch made me cry;
Tears welled up &I let out a sigh!

My leaves swayed,as if to thank her for this lease of life;
Thought, blessed is the man to have such a loving wife!

I then made a promise as in reverence;
To always brighten their life with my presence,
Let everyday, their windows open to an enchanting
view;
To, my purple blooms & glossy leaves, sun-kissed with
dew,

And since then in the backdrop I have been;
The nesting seasons , the chit -chat & first flights I have
seen,
I wait patiently & try to decipher;
The gossip, the discussion & the loving whisper,
Such tales of these ,then she strings, this lady dear;
And then paints bright pictures of livid colors &themes,
As if in wonderland, she is Alice in her dreams!
Come, let's all bask in the imagination she presents;
And drink & taste a little of life's essence!!

14. Hills & Highlands

These winding paths in the tranquil hills;
The lush green meadows & the rills,
The floating clouds, sliding past the blue sky;
The waterfalls & the meandering river running by,
Within its bed, these embedded pearls;
Narrate their story of shaping from boulders to pebbles,
In it, a lesson hidden for us all, to learn;
Many milestones, one must cross to achieve perfection,
All along the valley, the blue wild flowers on display;
As if bells are arranged in an array,
And U can almost hear the soothing tunes they play!
The pink & white blooms along the roadside;
 A refreshing treat to the weary eyes, this pretty sight!
 Makes the heart , leap & dance with delight!
Devbhoomi, a land of, idyllic panorama & rustic grace;
Sentinels of this mystique land ,these simple folks with
smiling face,
Pahadis, welcome everyone with open arms to this
majestic place;
A temple in the forest deep;
As a testimony of faith & belief,
With the Supreme , watching over us all;
Will surely hold our hand, before we fall!
And oh! These hilly nature trails ;

Are so incomplete without a few bird tales,
Saw a beautiful red faced, blue black bird, first thing in
the morn;
Khalij pheasant it was, rummaging on seeds at the break
of dawn,
Hopping on the rocks this violet bird with a yellow bill;
Spotting the Kastura or the blue whistling thrush, added
to the thrill,
And tucking all these, forever in to my heart's
scrapbook;
A kaleidoscope of memories in my soul I took,
Heading downhill, saw baya's nests swaying with the
gentle breeze;
As if, beckoning me to come back soon, for some more
stories!!

15. Story Of Seeds, Creepers & Climbers!!

Sleeping in the soil ,these dormant seeds;
For some water & sunshine they plead,
Some spring on their own ,these climbers wild;
Probably,God added them to our world , to keep us beguiled,
Some sown on purpose to spread the clan;
With of course ,some flowers & fruits in the plan,
Seeds sown, now a journey begins;
Seeing them sprout ,Oh!what joy it brings,
First the cotyledons so green ,appear;
Then the tendrils, as coils, it begins to bear,
'Lend me a helping hand & see me climb, dear,'
You can almost hear the tendril say, if you are near,
'A little', they keep growing day by day ;
Soon pretty flowers will be on display,
Next the entire mesh will be covered with greens;
As if the climber is spreading it's wings,
Turning the soil a little-a little pruning;
With your plants, sets your tuning,
A few more days and lo& behold!
The first gourd begins to peep from the leaf- folds,
Said the climber to me,'Go enjoy the fruits of labour;
It is an award for you to savour",

Just promise 'You'll tend to me;
And I'll submit my fruits to thee,
With my cart full of goodies & heart singing with pride;
Thanking the climbers ,I took an onward stride!!

16. The Hornbill Love Story

!

This huge fig tree in front of my home;
Upon which a hundred birds freely roam,
Among others, a pair of grey hornbills too it housed;
With a shrill cry their arrival was announced ,
This story began last summer in a way;
These intriguing creatures white and grey;
Drew my attention everyday,
Their signature heavy beaks and the casque;
Fascinated me and how? do not ask!

Believe you me to get a female's attention ;
In the bird world too is quite a tension,

Wooing the lady everyday with a new gift ;
Who in vain , at first did not give any lift !
Everyday it would proudly march up to the girl;
Flap its wings and do the twirl,
With a seed , lizard or a worm firmly tucked in it beak;
But the daring male continued the technique,
Finally , the female obliged and the male won her heart ;
Signalling me, that a family now, will soon start,
Love was in the air I could see;
A cavity was being cleaned up on the tree,

Their pecking ,necking and jostling,their love so carefree;
Their hopping from branch to branch with so much glee,
A final kiss and the female stepped in to the dome ;
Where she will bear and rear her chicks,Oh home sweet
home !
Now the dashing male had to do his best ;
Sealing the cavity with droppings and mud was quite a
test,
Once done, a little opening in the cavity was left ;
And till the eggs hatch and chicks grow, this is where its
beloved would rest,
Everyday many rounds the male made to and fro ,to
supply the food;
And this is how he looked after the brood,
Days changed in to months until one fine day;
Perched on the tree were two babies ,as if on display,
Brimming with pride the parents too were along ;
And all that I could hear , was a a happy family song,
The parents then gave them lessons on take off and
landing;
Preparing them for life just as we do for life's
understanding,
 I would put some morsels for them each day;
They had started trusting me in a way,
The chicks too started coming along;
And with me, their bond became a little more strong,

Soon one day the kids bid adieu;
In search of other fig trees and pastures they flew,
And the two hornbills were left behind ;
But Alas! destiny had other plans for them in mind,
somewhere up the tree ,the black kite lay in wait;
Death was lurking on the grey hornbill and its mate,

As the female had moulted feathers ,was an easy prey;
and with it's fate sealed ,it awaited doomsday,

On a fateful day the kite swooped down and clutched the
wife;
The male fluttered and cluttered to save its life,
The shrill cries and wails almost tore my heart;
but little could I do to save their world from ,falling
apart,
Then the gloom descended on the male ;
And began the solitary grey hornbill's tale,
Everyday I wished for a miracle to happen;
Seasons changed and again it was summer's turn;
The big ,fig tree had fresh new leaves and the birds were
on the run,

A few joyous ,shrill calls drew my attention one day;
And there on the branch ,with a new partner was the

hornbill grey!
It tapped on my window as if, to show me its new mate;
My happiness knew no bounds to see , its happy fate,
A connect for sure was there with me, I felt from within;
The birds too notice us and count us in ,
I thanked God Almighty as I looked up towards the sky;
He thinks for us all and upon him, we can rely ,
Once again the"book of life ", was adding a new chapter;
Hoping the Hornbills would live happily ever after!!

17. *A New Dawn's Journey*

In the quiet of morning, as the sun starts to rise;
With a heart full of dreams and excitement in your eyes:
The suitcases packed, with memories and more;
Today marks the moment you step out the door:

Tiny footsteps that once were so unsure ;
Now stride with purpose, so ...so mature:
A childhood of laughter, of lessons, and play ;

 As you turn your life's page in a brand new way:
 The room so empty yet so full it looks ;
  With some scattered combs, brushes , candles, some
lotions & in the shelf ,some books :
  Red slippers , medals, pink curtains and some toys so
old ;
  Will carry your fragrance & these things we will with
fondness behold :

Your parents taught you the letters, the numbers, the art;
But the biggest lesson was to follow your heart:
 As you explore the wild- wide world;

Embrace all its wonders & let your spirit be unfurled:

The echoes of laughter will linger in space;
But now you'll create your own magic at your pace:
With a smile on your face, and hope in your heart;
 Undaunted you may set on a smooth start :

And in the stillness, when shadows grow long ;
Hear the whispers of the loved, like an ever-familiar
song:
Though distance may stretch, as you've gone afar;
You carry our blessings, you're our shining star:

So go, girl go, let your journey unfold;
In the chapters of life, let your story be bold:
For, home is a heartbeat, wherever you go;
 Their wishes & blessings will surely follow!!

17.

Sighting of the Jacobin Cuckoo ,is the harbinger;
Monsoons are soon approaching ,it whispers,
Mythology too, has a mention of Jacobin's name;
In Kalidasa's Meghadoot, as" Chataka"it has earned its
fame,
A ray of hope for the farmer's standing crops;
The parched land eager to soak in ,the raindrops,
Let peace seep in to you , this rain ;
Let the child in you, bloom once again,
Remember! the paper boats we made & then set them
sail!
Watching ,who the winner would be at the end of the
trail?
The deliberate splash in the puddle & the wet shoes;
The almost brown shirts& forgotten mother's don'ts &
do's ,
O man! Awaken from the melee of life & notice;
The misty windows,bearing the impression of the
breathing breeze;
The clouds hanging low ,as if hugging & kissing the
trees,
The earthy scent of the soil after the first showers of
rain;

Which ,then will forever in your senses remain,
The magnificent changing shades of the skies;
Such a blissful treat to man's tired eyes,
 Mushrooms & wild daisies decorate the earth;
As if announcing & rejoicing ,their birth,
The rain-kissed flowers & the sparkling greener grass;
Drops holding on to the tip of leaves & unpredictable showers,
Let these sparkles hold on to your hair too;
Dance In the rain &let romance sweep you two,
Its time, to rediscover the lost- you, in this hullabaloo;
Do these little things often , that a child would do,
Let the soul breathe, rejoice & refresh itself;
Take out & read that book , lying for so long, on the shelf,
With my black diary & old melodies playing in the background;
Sipping hot cuppa & some fries, gives me joy profound,
Give an ear to the-pitter-patter of the raindrops & see, what they have to say?
They say,"We make music while you dance your way!".
Build some memories & tuck them in your heart;
These rainy days will help you ,make a good start,
For you to rewind & look back one day ;
Blessed were you to have lived that way!
Live life & enjoy simple pleasures as it is cascading so fast ;

Coz, your goodness, noble deeds & memories only ,will forever ,last!!

18. Memoirs of Chalkuria- A village

Nestled somewhere amidst the tall pine trees;
 where clouds swing in a skylike, trapeze,
   Where wildflowers adorn the earth and birds freely
roam;
lies a small village, Chalkuria, my mother's ancestral
home.
I accompanied my parents this time, for the Annual fest;
And without a doubt, this journey was one of the best!
Far away from the maddening crowd and the grind;
A healing balm this was for the soul and mind.
From across the globe come together these brethren;
The clan, their sons, daughters, and grandchildren,
To invoke Kuldevi's blessings for the good of all
mankind;
To celebrate and further strengthen the bond that binds.
And for me, the twinkle in my mother's eyes;
Was the crux of this emprise,
As she walked down her memory lane;
I could see she'd become a child again,
"Under this tree, my mother used to bathe me, she said,"
"And this is the route to school, as kids we tread",
These simple memories made her face radiate and her

feet did dance;
And I, walked beside her, soaking all this as if in a
trance!
The lessons learned were many for me
In villages, life is tough, u see!
But every face has a smile as the soul is free;
Where little is more and contentment is the key,
As a kid, I had heard of folktales and folklore about this
goddess
 Long ago had escaped from a Rohilla prince, this
Nandadevi princess.
And merged with the holy mountains forever;
Still standing tall, these peaks Nanda & Sunanda, her
sister,
In awe was I, of palanquin of this goddess;
All was surreal as if magical powers possessed,
The games, the dances, the songs and the laughter;

Meeting elders and visiting Kuldevi thereafter
Up and down the hill my mother thronged
 Like a kid, she was, all strings attached to where she
belonged,
With a lifetime of memories, we headed back;
 The mind and soul satiated, we hit the track!!

19. Cottage Of My Dreams

A few wooden planks by the stream;
Lead to this cosy cottage of my dreams ,
Where the crimson sun bidding adieu;
Fills up the sky with its hues ,
Overflowing the fields and the moor ;
Wild pansies and daisies which surely lure,
Where the yellow bells on tiny green trees ;
Tinkle and chime gently with the breeze,
Where ,the hills and the valleys beyond ;
bathe in these shades and form a bond,
Where, resides a sea of hope and the spirit is free;
Where clouds, like cotton balls spread , till the eyes can
see;
The birds returning to their nests;
To hold their babies close to the breasts,
There is silence everywhere ;
But still there is so much to hear,
ITo the cottage ,I head back from my walk ;
Andon the paper, let my brushes do the talk,
Very close to the actual ones I get
But creator of course , is the artist at its best!
Another day will soon arise
Unfolding nature's new surprise!

20. The Dandelion Lesson

Dry seeds , flowers & feathery bristles blow away;
With the wind,they twist & turn & sway,
The strong ones catch on , hold & stay;
All this, my friends is not in vain!
But to sprout ,bloom & blossom again;
This is what nature teaches;
Dare you have to ! it preaches,
One must stand up & fight all odds in life;
Coz, only the fittest in body & soul will survive!
Little did we know, there hid a profound meaning in the seeds,
We called, budiya ke baal & collected as kids;
The dandelion & the cottonwood seeds are here ,to remind,
Take a resolve to put your fears & failures behind,
In testing times stay strong, the tides will surely turn,
Although ,with new norms life will once again be, on the run;
Each day ,the sun goes down to come up again;
The spring is predecessor of the rains,
Buds waiting to unfurl their petals, to a new season;
Chicks flutter their wings for a reason,
Butterflies so fragile, still so agile;
Metamorphosis from within! how beautifully they

compile,
There is a time to reap & a time to sow;
 A time to learn & a time to grow,
All pieces fall in place,the nature's jigsaw, is such designed;
A place for you ,a place for me is already assigned,
Then why the hurry , cacophony & malice spoil our heart?
Let's all cleanse our souls &make a fresh new start,
"Less of me & more of We" might just make the Earth ;
A place to live & a life lived worth!!

21. Live Life awhile !

Live Life, awhile !
We all are on borrowed time here;
Nothing permanent to hold and stare,
Like grains of sand sifting away;
Nearing our end ,day by day,
Let the rainbows please you a little ;
Let the rain - kissed rose appease you a little,
And let the colors of the sky seap in ;
To heal the wounds from within,
Let the flowers, the wind and sunshine ;
Make your heart a little divine ,
The pets ,the birds and the butterflies;
Will cover the rest and suffice,
The things you would need to travel forth;
Once you head way beyond the North,
Remnants of these little things willshow;
How much you lived ,before you go ,
So grab a little basket and start collecting
No worldly things but these little blessings!!

www.ingramcontent.com/pod-product-compliance
Lightning Source LLC
LaVergne TN
LVHW021251200726
843509LV00012B/1639